CLASH OF THE CRYPTIDS

LIZARD MAN VS. THE SWAMP MONSTER

by Golriz Golkar

CAPSTONE PRESS
a capstone imprint

Published by Capstone Press, an imprint of Capstone
1710 Roe Crest Drive, North Mankato, Minnesota 56003
capstonepub.com

Library of Congress Cataloging-in-Publication Data
Names: Golkar, Golriz, author.
Title: Lizard Man vs. the Swamp Monster / by Golriz Golkar.
Other titles: Lizard Man versus the Swamp Monster
Description: North Mankato, Minnesota : Capstone Press, an imprint of Capstone, [2026] | Series: Clash of the cryptids | Includes bibliographical references and index. | Audience: Ages 9–11 | Audience: Grades 4–6 | Summary: "A tall, green creature stands on one side of the road. His red eyes glow. A tall, hairy creature stands on the other side of the road. His yellow eyes glow. Suddenly, they pounce! It's Lizard Man against the Swamp Monster! Readers can compare each creature's characteristics, histories, and behaviors to determine which cryptid will win in this hi-lo book." — Provided by publisher.
Identifiers: LCCN 2025002809 (print) | LCCN 2025002810 (ebook) | ISBN 9798875225840 (hardcover) | ISBN 9798875225796 (paperback) | ISBN 9798875225802 (pdf) | ISBN 9798875225819 (epub) | ISBN 9798875225826 (kindle edition)
Subjects: LCSH: Monsters—Juvenile literature. | Swamps—Miscellanea—Juvenile literature.
Classification: LCC GR825 .G575 2026 (print) | LCC GR825 (ebook) | DDC 398.21—dc23/eng/20250210
LC record available at https://lccn.loc.gov/2025002809
LC ebook record available at https://lccn.loc.gov/2025002810

Editorial Credits
Editor: Ashley Kuehl; Designer: Hilary Wacholz; Media Researcher: Rebekah Hubstenberger; Production Specialist: Tori Abraham

Image Credits
Getty Images: ClickAndPray Photography, 9 (background), David Wall, 24–25; Shutterstock: Daniel Eskridge, cover, 5, 6, DM7, 9 (lizard man), gnepphoto, 29 (medal), JM-MEDIA, 10–11, 19, 20–21, PHOTOCREO Michal Bednarek, 13, Ralf Juergen Kraft, 7, Rollercoastershark, 15, tsuneomp, 17, 23, 26, 27, 29 (lizard man), Vac1, 12

Design Elements
Shutterstock: AlyonaZhitnaya, Ballerion, Katarinanh

Printed and bound in China. 006276

TABLE OF CONTENTS

Words in **bold** are in the glossary.

A BIG, WET BATTLE

It is a foggy evening. Lizard Man walks out from the trees. His eyes glow red. He flashes his sharp-clawed hands.

Suddenly, another two-legged creature appears. The Swamp Monster has a dark, hairy body. His glowing yellow eyes stare at Lizard Man. The Swamp Monster lets out a shrill cry.

It's one **cryptid** against another. Who will win the battle?

Name: South Carolina Lizard Man

Alias: Lizard Man of Scape Ore Swamp

Type of Cryptid: Lizard-like, **humanoid**

First Sighting: 1988

Range (Area): South Carolina

Likes: Scaring people, attacking cars

Dislikes: Being disturbed

Name: Honey Island Swamp Monster

Aliases: Louisiana's Bigfoot, Bayou Beast

Type of Cryptid: Humanoid, ape-like, alligator-like

First Sighting: 1963

Range (Area): Louisiana

Likes: Wading in water and eating boar

Dislikes: Being around people

A LITTLE HISTORY

Lizard Man was first spotted in 1988. A teen boy was changing a tire on a dark road. Suddenly, a huge green creature came running straight at him. The boy jumped into his car. But the creature leaped on top! It finally let go when the car swerved. Later, the creature was gone. But the claw marks stayed on the car!

The Honey Island Swamp Monster story is even stranger. **Cajun folktales** tell of a lost child who wandered into a swamp. He was raised by alligators. Then he grew up into the Swamp Monster. The meat-eating cryptid lived in the water and on land.

That's not the only legend, though. Another story tells of a circus train. It crashed in the Honey Island area in the 1900s. Chimpanzees escaped into the woods around the swamp. An alligator and a chimpanzee had a child. He became the Swamp Monster.

A LOT ALIKE

Many people say Lizard Man is half man and half lizard. He is a tall **bipedal** cryptid. He has green, scaly skin. Each hand has clawed fingers. Each foot has clawed toes.

7 feet (2.1 meters) tall
Red eyes
Clawed fingers
Two legs
Clawed toes
Green, scaly skin

The Swamp Monster is tall too. He walks on two feet. He has a humanoid face. His body is covered in black hair. His big feet are **webbed**. Some have heard him scream!

7 feet (2.1 m) tall
Yellow eyes
Clawed fingers
Dark, hairy body
Two legs
Big, webbed feet

WHERE THEY HIDE

Lizard Man lurks in shadows. He scares people and damages cars. After the first reported sighting, more South Carolina residents came forward. They said that their car bumpers had been damaged. The bumpers had been chewed up or torn off.

Local police also found large, three-toed footprints in the mud. Many news reporters came to the area. They hoped to spot the cryptid. In 2015, a woman took a photo of the cryptid walking near the woods. A man filmed it walking in a swamp. But people were not sure this proof was real.

A STINKY MESS

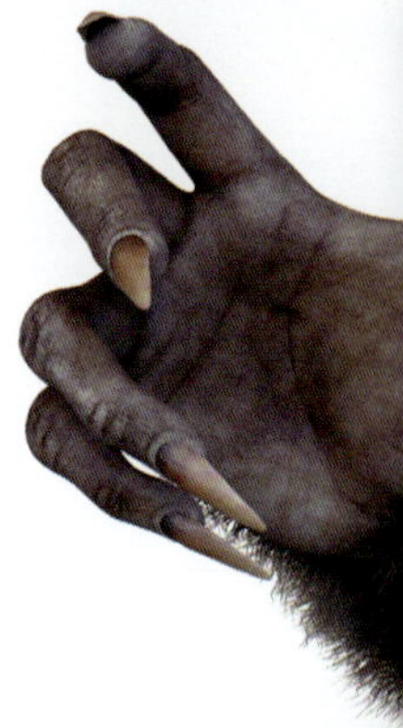

The Swamp Monster is a hungry meat-eater. He tears up camps, looking for food. The first known sighting happened in 1963. Two men were camping in the woods when they spotted a smelly creature eating a dead boar. When the creature heard them, he stood up like a human. He stared at them and then ran away.

The men later returned to that spot. They found boar remains and large, three-toed footprints. They took a **cast** of the footprints. One of the men later filmed the cryptid lurking in the woods. Was it really the Swamp Monster? It's still a mystery!

FACT

In 1988, a radio station offered a $1 million reward for the Swamp Monster's capture. But it was never claimed.

AN EPIC FIGHT

Lizard Man stretches out his arms. His clawed hands reach high above his head. The Swamp Monster drools as his eyes grow wide.

Lizard Man pounces on the Swamp Monster. He digs his claws into the monster's body. The Swamp Monster screams in pain. But Lizard Man doesn't let go.

The Swamp Monster finally manages to wiggle away. He runs to the swamp. He leaps into the water with a shriek.

IT'S OVER! LIZARD MAN WINS!

DO YOU AGREE? Who do you think would win when

Lizard Man and the Swamp Monster CLASH?

GLOSSARY

bipedal (by-PEH-duhl)—walking on two legs

Cajun (KAY-juhn)—people in southern Louisiana whose French-speaking ancestors moved from what is now Nova Scotia in Canada

cast (CAST)—an impression taken from an object that keeps the object's form

cryptid (KRIP-tid)—a creature whose existence has not been proven

folktale (FOHK-tale)—stories told and passed down by a group of people over many years

humanoid (HYOO-muh-noyd)—having human features

webbed (WEBD)—connected by tissues or membranes, such as on fingers and toes

READ MORE

Erickson, Marty. *The Loch Ness Monster*. Mankato, MN: The Child's World, 2022.

Finn, Peter. *Do Monsters Exist?* New York: Gareth Stevens Publishing, 2023.

Respicio, Mae. *Tracking Cryptids with Tech*. Mankato, MN: Pebble, 2024.

INTERNET SITES

Atlas Obscura: International Cryptozoology Museum
atlasobscura.com/places/international-cryptozoology-museum

City of Bishopville: The Lizard Man of Scape Ore Swamp
cityofbishopvillesc.com/the-lizard-man/

Mississippi Gulf Coast National Heritage Area: Honey Island Swamp Monster
msgulfcoastheritage.ms.gov/flavorful/people/honey-island-swamp-monster/

Pearson: 10 Creepy Cryptids You Should Know About
pearson.com/languages/en-us/community/blogs/2023/10/english-cryptids.html

INDEX

ABOUT THE AUTHOR

Golriz Golkar is the author of more than 40 nonfiction books for children. Inspired by her work as an elementary school teacher, she loves to write the kinds of books that students are excited to read. Golriz holds a B.A. in American literature and culture from UCLA and an Ed.M. in language and literacy from the Harvard Graduate School of Education. She loves to travel and study languages. Golriz lives in France with her husband and young daughter, Ariane. She thinks children are the very best teachers, and she loves learning from her daughter every day.